The Hidden Curriculum

The Hidden Curriculum

Life Lessons
You Won't Learn
in a Classroom

DR. RUBIN COCKRELL

Dr. Rubin Cockrell
P.O. Box. 292753
Nashville, TN 37229

rcockrell@imagepositive.com
facebook.com/rubin.cockrell
twitter.com/rubincockrell

UNLOCK THE CHAMPION

© 2010 Unlock the Champion, Inc.

All rights reserved.
No part of this work may be reproduced or transmitted in any form or by any means, electronic or mechanical, including photocopying and recording, or by any information storage or retrieval system, except as may be expressly permitted by the Unlock the Champion 1976 Copyright Act or in writing from the publisher. Requests for permission should be e-mailed to info@imagepositive.com or mailed to P.O. Box 292753, Nashville, TN 37229

Unless otherwise noted, Scripture quotations are from the King James version of the Bible.

Printed in Canda

Book and Cover Design by Ken M. Strickland

Contents

Introduction 7

1. Life is a Hustle 11

2. Thinking Without Boxes 43

3. Learn to Lead Yourself so that
   You Can Lead Others 65

4. Tolerated to Celebrated 83

5. Staying Ready 99

Introduction

Who really cares about the curriculum that we have to learn in school? I mean, as long as I come to class, listen, and memorize the material, I will be prepared for the school of life. As long as I study hard or even just show up, I am prepared to be successful in life. Right? I can drop out of school, set up shop pushing illegal substances and quickly make more money than the person who was trying to persuade me to stay within the classroom.

This is the interesting thought process that a lot of people believe until they enter the school of life and receive their first test, without time to study. You receive all this education or lack of education and then the teacher called Dr. Life steps into your classroom. What are you going to do then? Are you going to show up late, make an excuse about your homework or complain that you're ready to go home?

This book was written to examine life lessons you won't learn in the classroom that will shape, mold and guide you for the ultimate class called life. Many times within our lives, we have those life experiences that can either become stepping stones or stumbling blocks. It's what we learn from those experiences that will mold and guide us for the near future.

Introduction

I want to encourage you that no matter what is happening in your life presently, the best is yet to come. Through your test you create your own personal testimony to share with and help others. So keep your head up and keep moving.

My sole purpose in writing this book is to educate, enrich and enhance your life. If this book can help you to achieve your overall goals, then I will achieve my personal goals. This book will reach those from the street to the elite, the classroom to the boardroom.

"Failure is not an option. Excuses are unacceptable. Excellence must be our way of life."

—Dr. Rubin Cockrell

Dr. Rubin Cockrell is a professor at several colleges within the Tennessee region. Dr. Cockrell teaches within the Business/Education departments of those institutions. He also serves as CEO of Positive Images & Associates, a firm that specializes in educational leadership, empowerment, and management consulting. In his role with the Nashville, TN-based company, Dr. Cockrell trains business leaders, college students, and church groups to implement tools for achieving excellence and quality productivity within their lives and their organizations all across the country.

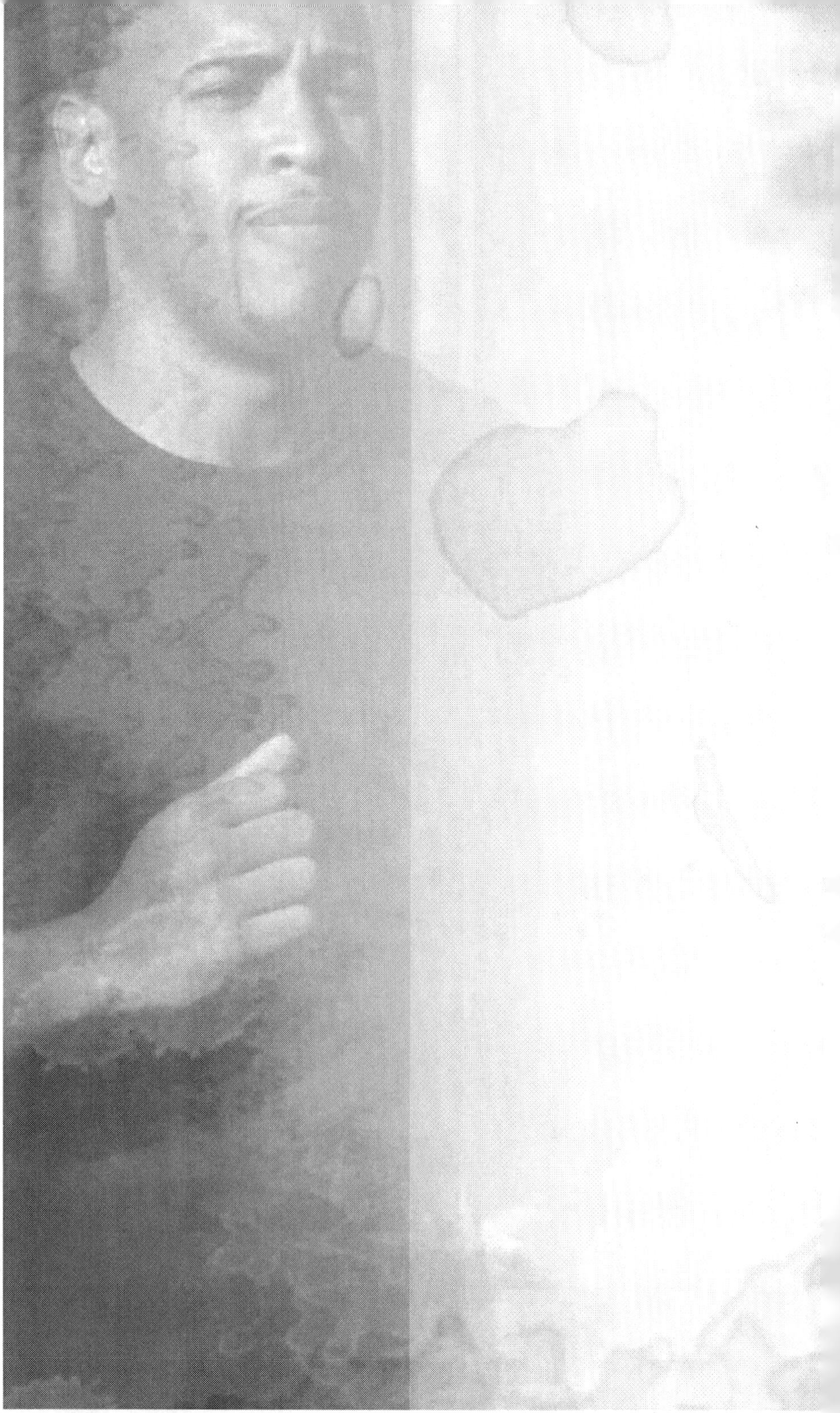

Chapter 1
Life is a Hustle

The word hustle brings forth negative thoughts within our society. By definition, hustle means to push or force one's way, jostle or shove; to obtain by aggressive or illicit means; to beg, solicit, or swindle. I take a different perspective with these meanings. Think about when you wake up every day trying to get your kids up, trying to go to school, or get yourself prepared for work. You do this not necessarily to compete against others in the classroom or at work, but to compete against everyday society. Thus, in essence, you are hustling. You are hustling to perform in your job, to be the best you can be! Hustle also means to be aggressive, especially in business or other financial dealings; to convey or cause to move; to urge, produce, or speed up. Therefore, with this new frame of reference, life is a hustle. You must move forward with a sense of urgency.

Why move forward with urgency? It is through this momentum that you move not necessarily for speed, but to produce the most efficient and productive movements possible. These are the

The Hidden Curriculum

concepts and ideas that you will not be taught in a classroom, but that are learned through the trials and tribulations of life. Keep in mind, you can be overly prepared, be at the top of the class in grade performance, and be financially secure; however, you can still be knocked on your butt. Through these life lessons, you get teachable moments. You must realize that life's scenarios can either be stepping stones or stumbling blocks. What determines this is what we allow, our perspective, and our attitude. You have to move forward with a sense of urgency. Abraham Lincoln once said, "Good things come to those who wait." I would add this to that famous quote, "Those who wait get the leftovers of those who hustle."

The Art of Hustling

You have to hustle mentally, physically, emotionally, and spiritually at all times and for all of your life. The minute you get complacent with life, in relationships, and with yourself, the rug will be pulled out from under you. Thomas Holdcroft stated, "Life is a grindstone. Whether it grinds us down or polishes us up depends on us." How you react to these situations is very telling of your character and maturity level. Many good people wonder why bad things continue to happen to them. Let's put a different perspective on this scenario. Shari Barr said, "Expecting life to treat you well because you are a good person is like expecting an angry bull not to charge because you are a vegetarian." It is the difficult times that mold us into the person we are to become. Think about a lump of coal. Over thousands of years, as coal gets compressed and pushed, it evolves into a diamond. For this beautiful creation to come about and get that result, it has to be put under unimaginable pressure for years.

In order to understand mental fitness, you must first understand what that encompasses. It includes intelligence, perceptions, and attitude. Life's essential goal is for you to use all of your intelligence and potential to be all that you can be. A psychologist by the name of Abraham Maslow, developed a theory of a hierarchy of needs. There are five levels of needs; physiological, safety & security, recognition, self-esteem, and self-actualization. According to his theory, the lower level needs must be met first before the higher needs can be met and satisfied. The reason I cite this theory is because in order to achieve true happiness you must possess the confidence and personal power of knowing who you are and what you want to achieve. You cannot move forward if you haven't met your basic needs first.

The Hidden Curriculum

Furthermore, you cannot move forward if you are filled with trepidation and fear.

The oldest and strongest emotion that we feel is fear. An old expression says, "When you look mentally, a fear comes over you." Fear deteriorates us from the inside out. We must learn to face our fear and conquer it. Nelson Mandela once said, "The brave man is not he who does not feel afraid, but he who conquers that fear." Conversely, Michael Ignatieff said, "Living fearlessly is not the same thing as never being afraid. It's good to be afraid occasionally. Fear is a great teacher." It is out of fear and doubt from which come the greatest triumphs. Susan Piver stated, "Fearlessness requires attention and receptivity—it takes focus to stand in the still eye of a tornado and not be swept away by it." Sometimes the hardest thing to do is be still, so you can observe, listen, understand, contemplate, concentrate, reflect, and then take action.

Know yourself and understand your hustle

Additionally, each of us has our own perceptions, needs, and unique set of abilities. Intelligence used to be measured by a standard IQ test. However, Thomas Armstrong, author of *7 Kinds of Smart: Identifying and Developing Your Many Intelligences*, and Howard Gardner, author of *Frames of the Mind:*

The Theory of Multiple Intelligences, helped us to redefine our views on intelligence. **Eight levels of intelligence** have been defined:

Word smart – These individuals have verbal/linguistic intelligence. They like to read, talk, and write about information. They have a proven ability to argue, persuade, entertain, and teach with words.

Picture smart – These individuals have spatial intelligence. They love to draw, sketch, and visualize information. They can perceive information in three-dimensional spaces and can recreate various aspects of our visual world.

Logic smart – These individuals have logical/mathematical intelligence. They like logic, numbers, riddles, and puzzles. The have a strong ability to reason and solve problems. They think in terms of cause and effect and love to explore patterns and relationships.

Musical smart – These individuals have melody and rhythm intelligence. They can keep time with music and have the ability to appreciate, perceive, and produce rhythms.

Body smart – These individuals have kinesthetic and physical intelligence. They can understand and control their bodies. They have tactile sensitivity, like to move, and can handle objects quite skillfully.

The Hidden Curriculum

Outdoor smart – These individuals have environmental intelligence. They have the ability to measure, observe, and chart plants and animals. They like to participate in outdoor activities, keep journals, and collect and classify.

Self-smart – These individuals have inner and intrapersonal intelligence. They have the ability to be contemplative, introspective, and are self-disciplined.

People smart – These individuals have interpersonal intelligence. They have a great insight and ability to understand other people. They like to talk. They are very responsive to moods, intentions, and desires of other people.

You can have several different types of intelligence along this scale. You don't have to be the smartest to succeed in life. Throughout the world, several CEOs never graduated from college. What makes them successful is their candid ability to move forward, to have a vision, and their ability to take action. They realized it was time for them to look at the clouds of opportunity and not the fog of complacency. Each CEO also had the ability to move forward and came to the realization of getting on with the business of moving their vision forward (hustling).

Are you emotionally fit? Do you have yourself in gear? Do you think good thoughts about yourself and about others? Have you addressed past hurts, problems with parents, friends, business partners, and significant others? If you haven't addressed these issues, it does affect your ability to get out and hustle for achievement and excellence on the ladder of life. Are you mentally and emotionally ready to reevaluate many aspects of your life? A positive attitude and high self-esteem are extremely important. However, if your beliefs and perceptions are misguided, neither will help you reach your goals. Mind shifts and attitude adjustments are often necessary to see things differently with keen and new understanding and perspective. Ask yourself this question: Attitudes are contagious; is mine worth catching today? The old adage that one bad apple spoils the whole bunch is extremely accurate. A person with a great attitude can affect a room and, adversely, so can a person with a bad attitude. If you haven't addressed past hurts, you will have a wounded attitude ultimately clouding the judgment of the leadership realm in which you are encapsulated; be it the church (wounded ministry and wounded leaders), business (wounded organization and wounded administrators, wounded staff), or personally (wounded spirit and reactions). This will affect your ability to get out and do what you need to do to move forward in society in a healthy way.

The Hidden Curriculum

The emotional hustle

People are brought into our life for a season, season(s), and lifetimes. There are some people you are going to have to drop off by the wayside because they are extra cargo on your ship. These people keep you from moving forward or hustling in life to move yourself or others forward. When you don't take time out to have accountability toward your hustle and do what you need to do, you will sink like a ship. A ship can sink in two ways: either because it has too much cargo on the boat or the water pressure slowly overtakes the boat and it capsizes.

Having too much cargo on the ship puts you over capacity. When you are over capacity, then that boat starts to sink quickly because you have too much weight; whether it is the weight of people, the weight of dead opportunities, or the weight of goals and objectives you go after that are not your passions and dreams. They are just things for your own self-motives or going after areas that aren't in your purpose. Many people just try to keep up with the Joneses. This is the cargo you must let go of and move off of your ship. Once you are able to lighten your ship, you can think more clearly about your hustle.

A slowly sinking ship is often more detrimental and harder to detect. Often, we do not or will not address past hurts. Incidents that happened early in your childhood or areas in your adult life that have affected you on a personal level often cause you trepidation or cause you to react with a wounded spirit. You must be willing to look at, face, and move past prior infractions, misdeeds, and injustices.

The mental hustle

Do you take time out to address those mental areas within your life that continue to have a stronghold on you and keep you from your peace and freedom? If you don't consistently take the time to address, overcome, and forgive these injustices, your ship will surely sink.

The old adage states, "If you always do what you've always done, you will always get what you always got. You will never be able to move forward and have the hustle of life. As you swell with emotions of hurt, betrayal, anguish, sorrow, etc, the walls of your ship begin to expand from stress, the nuts and bolts that hold the body of the ship together become squeaky, because they haven't been oiled and properly maintained. Water starts seeping into the holes. As a result, the ship starts sinking little by little until it has taken on so much water that it has no other alternative but to sink from the weight and pressure. This is your wake up

The Hidden Curriculum

call. So are you sinking? Fast? Slowly? This all affects your ability to hustle throughout the course of life. It is very important that you address these issues and take some of the weight off of your shoulders. You should react from a place of peace and grace, not from a place of hurt and fear.

The physical hustle

Now that you understand your mental fitness, do you understand the impact and necessity of being physically fit? Do you take the time to work out or to put the proper foods in your body? Do you get proper rest? Are you physically fit for the challenge of leading people and for the challenge of understanding your own vision and dream? Being prepared physically is one of the most basic and fundamental of your needs. Without the proper rest and nutrition, you can not excel and be at your best. Lack of rest and nutrition can lead to an array of health issues including depression, fatigue, stress, temperament issues, diabetes, heart trouble, high blood pressure, etc. You owe it to yourself to take care of yourself. Don't let everyone else's needs, wants, and desires overshadow your own. It doesn't make you selfish, weak, or a bad person to take care of yourself first. It is a necessity.

Life is a Hustle

The spiritual hustle

Are you prepared spiritually? I'm not talking about reading the Bible or attending church every Sunday morning. Are you being that spiritual light to yourself, your family, and friends; not necessarily by what you say but by what you do? Are you being the man or woman that God has called you to be in society? This is something that you have to look at on a one-on-one basis. Sometimes the hardest thing to do is be still, to wait, to have patience and to let go, giving all your glory to the man who gave it all to us. It is equally hard to remember to be thankful for what you do have and not the things you don't have. Be vigilant in your prayer and be willing to receive a message, even if it's not what you want to hear.

It's time to make your next move your best move

Once you have prepared yourself mentally, emotionally, physically, and spiritually, the next step is to find your passion. Ask yourself this question: What is the one thing that I would be willing to do even if I did not get paid or what is the thing that I do so well that people are willing to pay me for that talent? The answer to these questions is what passion is. Passion is a strong or extravagant fondness, enthusiasm, or desire for anything. It gives you the ability to go above and beyond.

The Hidden Curriculum

Furthermore, it gives you the confidence to not make excuses about why you are not achieving certain goals and objectives.

If you are not sure what I mean, think about this example. People talk about drug dealers and how they are bad for communities and citizens. Ironically, drug dealers have one of the best work ethics and have a strong passion for what they do. Think about it; because of their passion to make money, they get out there and hustle whether it is raining, sleeting, or snowing to achieve their goals. No excuses, they will put their family, significant others, and friends, all to the side because they are passionate about reaching one common goal – making money. I am not endorsing nor condoning what they do. I am simply trying to show that passion can drive you to do certain things; be it positive or negative. If one could take the same type of work ethic of the drug dealer and put it toward something constructive and positive, what amazing things one could get done.

I guarantee that if you realize what you are passionate about, your outcome and ability to hustle will improve by leaps and bounds. Keep in mind; you will have different passions at different stages and ages within your life. This is due in part to normal transitions of maturity and due to different trials and tribulations that you have experienced. Know that you have found what you are passionate about. You must realize that passion sometimes helps you to create the why.

Why do you do what you do day-to-day, month-to-month, and year-to-year? Are you focused on what you do? Why are you focused on what you do? Take some time to examine these questions. Start by creating a checklist. By doing this, you can put into perspective what your motives are, what your needs are, as well as what your wants are.

Reviewing this checklist on a day-to-day basis will help you understand if you are moving toward your passion or taking a step back. The key is relying on utilizing the list you have created and keeping your vision in front of you. Thus, you must keep that list with you. Actually having several copies is necessary. I keep a list in my notebook, in my bedroom, in the car, and yes, even in the bathroom. By having multiple copies in multiple areas, you are holding yourself accountable. Additionally, through developing your passions, you will develop the ability to hustle toward your goals and, ultimately, allow yourself to do what you need to do to achieve your goals and your passions. This step is very important.

Vision is an important component of hustling. Vision is defined as the act or power of anticipating

The Hidden Curriculum

that which will or may come to be. When you have a vision for a goal and objective in life and you put that action step in place, then your vision can lead to your victory in life. Remember, another word for action is hustle and hustling is another word for putting action in place. You can have all of the goals and dreams in the world, but if you do not put your vision or hustle in place, you will not achieve those dreams. Joel Baker states, "Vision without action is just a dream. Action without vision is just passing time away. Action with vision is making a positive difference." If you choose not to make these changes, you will have a would-of, should-of, could-of attitude and years down the road you will try to live vicariously through your children. Unfortunately, this happens to many people within our society. There are three types of people in the world: 1) dreamers, 2) doers, and 3) dreamers and doers. I challenge you to find your vision and be the dreamer and the doer. This combination is the person who hustles and gets things accomplished.

The vision of your hustle

Once you have realized your vision, what do you do to get momentum to move to the next level? Keep in mind as you move forward in life, you can be a success and have monetary riches and still have issues arise. In today's economy, people are being laid off or downsized; even those individuals who have worked for a company for 20 to 30 years. We live in a time of instability and change. What separates people is how they embrace change and the attitude with which they address the change. Change happens unpredictably and inevitably. Alan Cohen summed up change in this manner, "It takes a lot of courage to release the familiar and seemingly secure, to embrace the new. But there is no real security in what is no longer meaningful. There is more security in the adventurous and exciting, for in movement there is life, and in change there is power." This is what hustling is all about. Thomas Edison said, "Everything comes to him who hustles while he waits". What he is trying to say is that, even in moments of silence and stillness, you should still be hustling with ideas and creativity.

Since change occurs daily and is often viewed as offensive and difficult, you must continually revise your vision. You should ask yourself often, what is my vision for myself? What is my vision for my family? What is my vision for my kids? Your first priority should be your vision for yourself because if you don't have that in place, then you will have major problems and will stagnate. There are core

The Hidden Curriculum

principles you must examine when you look at creating and modifying your vision on a daily basis.

Three core hustle principles

Principle 1: With vision comes intellectual capital, human capital, and social capital which ultimately translates into financial capital. You must realize that you don't know everything and can't do everything. As a result of your passion for your vision, you must master the human capital component. People are your greatest asset. If people see that you are passionate about vision, then they will take to your vision and be willing to help you. Warren Buffet once said, "The business schools reward difficult complex behavior more than simple behavior, but the simple behavior is more effective." This concept is very important. For leaders, it is more important to know the most important things than to know everything. As a result, you have to bring people forth to help you specifically in that process. Good leaders can't afford to be caught up in every little detail. If they do, they lose perspective and the ability to lead.

So what is your solution? Decide that it is okay that you don't have to know everything. You must invest in Human Capital. Surround yourself with people who excel in areas where you are weak.

Life is a Hustle

Amos Parrish says, "The best leaders are those most interested in surrounding themselves with assistants and associates smarter than they are. They are frank in admitting this and are willing to pay for such talents."

Principle 2: You must learn to work within your strengths and not focus on your weaknesses. By identifying your strengths and weaknesses, you become self-aware. Keep in mind that self-knowledge and self-awareness are the beginning of self-improvement. Larry Bossidy and Ram Charan stated, "Self-awareness gives you the capacity to learn from your mistakes as well as your successes. It enables you to keep growing." Benjamin Franklin said, "Observe all men. Thyself most." Thus, in an effort to indentify your strengths, you must realize that your strengths are your vantage point. Simply stated, you must learn to identify, understand, and develop your strengths. This will influence your success in school, career, and life. You can utilize your natural talents to build on your strengths. Talent is defined as "a naturally recurring pattern of thought, feeling or behavior that can be productively applied". Ability is defined as "what a person can specifically do". Thus, strength is defined as "the ability to provide consistent, near-perfect performance in a given activity". To put it plainly, it's your

The Hidden Curriculum

ability to perform a given task or function extremely well. Naturally, you start with dominant talents. Then, you refine them into strengths through knowledge, skills, and experience.

If you work within your strengths, then you can maximize your potential and strive to gather individuals around you who help you maintain and gather strength. You must realize that you will have to find people who excel at your weaknesses. A great leader understands this concept. Look at Warren Buffet, Steve Jobs, and Bill Gates. They embraced this concept. These visionary leaders brought people around them who were strong where they were weak in both business and life. The Bible says, "that a person's weakness will be your strengths and your strengths will be that person's weaknesses." Look at your spouse. This person should compliment you and you should compliment them. I'm not talking about niceties and sentiment; I'm referring to the strengths and weaknesses offsetting each other. Her strengths are your weaknesses and your strengths are her weaknesses. This simple concept is fundamentally important for you to move forward with vision and gather the tools to be successful in life.

Principle 3: You must take a very hard and fast look at what occupies your time. You cannot have a successful vision when you are spread too thin or in conflicting directions from your vision. What controls your time – school, kids, spouse, work, or recreational activities? Navigating life requires you to identify and know what your strengths are. You must make some tough decisions. Are you getting people around you who compliment your strengths and weaknesses? Are you stuck between moving forward or just being complacent? If so, you have got to identify mentors and accountability partners to push you to the next level. Don't limit yourself as a leader. Mentors can help you cultivate trust in others. If you don't have a mentor, then find someone to assist you in moving forward with your vision. Gail Devers states, "Keep your dreams alive, understand to achieve anything requires faith and belief in yourself, vision, hard work, determination, and dedication. Remember all things are possible for those who believe."

Mistakes are part of the hustle

When you look at your ability to hustle in life, at moving forward and creating a vision, understand that you will make mistakes. Hugh White says, "When you make a mistake, don't look back at it long. Take the reason of the thing into your mind and then look forward. Mistakes are lessons of

The Hidden Curriculum

wisdom. The past cannot be changed. The future is yet in your power. You must realize your mistakes and admit to your weaknesses. Show your vulnerability. Don't cause maximum damage and fail to admit. Don't be in a state of denial. This will cause issues for you as a leader. When it comes to success it's not the number of mistakes that you make; it's the number of times you make the same mistake." Mistakes show us what needs to be improved. Ponder this question for a moment: If we didn't make mistakes, how would we know what needed to be improved? Having the ability to recognize, admit to, correct, and learn from one's mistakes is a sign of growth and maturity. We must learn to accept our trials and tribulations as a blessing because it is through these that teachable moments come forth. These are life experiences and lessons that cannot and will not be taught in a classroom. This is the curriculum you learn in life that will move you forward. Insist on learning from your mistakes. The old adage, "if you always do what you always done, you will always get what you've always got", is quite accurate. You will get the same results if you continue to repeat the same mistakes.

People who try to avoid failure at all costs never learn and they end up repeating the same mistakes over and over again. An analogy would be the

Life is a Hustle

proverbial dog that continues to chase his own tail. Keep in mind, you attain great wisdom from success and success comes through mistakes and failure. What separates the good from the mediocre is your ability to get back up and continue to move forward. This is very important in leadership, in expounding your vision, and in maneuvering through life. While one person hesitates because he feels inferior, the other is busy making mistakes and becoming superior.

Take time for a self-check or you will hustle yourself

Ask yourself, what am I missing? Do I do a self-check on a daily basis? You can run and try to help this person and that person in order to not have to stop and deal with things. But in reality, we are keeping busy because we are not pleased with our own lives. When we aren't pleased with what is going on in our own lives we blame everyone else for our failures, such as the dog, girlfriend, wife, kids, husband, etc. It is important to figure out if you are a person who never takes ownership and blames everyone else. It is important that we look at ourselves and acknowledge our attitude towards the mistakes that we make. What type of attitude do you display? Do you have an open attitude to realize that you have made a mistake and you need to learn

The Hidden Curriculum

from your mistake? Or are you in a state of denial and blaming everybody else. Do you own up to your mistakes and take responsibility? If not, then it's important to start making the necessary changes. You must also ask yourself, who do I surround myself with? Who influences me? Are they good influences? What type of information am I getting from my mentors? How do they address their mistakes? You must watch the company that you keep. A true leader leads by example. Remember, sometimes people are placed in your life for a season. We have to learn when to let go. If not, then it's imperative to make the necessary changes so that you can make the right adjustments.

Life is a hustle and it requires action. You have to keep moving at all times and at all costs. Do what you must to move forward. If you get knocked down, pick yourself back up. If you see others get knocked down, help pick them up. You must have the ability to lift as you climb. As you move forth you must be willing to help others. This will help ensure your success and help carve a niche for yourself in society. "The difference between try and triumph is just a little umph!" Therefore, make sure to utilize all of your umph while you are hustling in life.

Keep in mind that behind every hustle there is a reason why you do what you do. Know that or those reason(s)!! This will increase your work stamina and effort to complete tasks and goals that lie in front of you. This will also help you to become disciplined about how you go through your everyday experiences. I remember when I was working on completing my doctoral degree. One major motivation was simply to use the degree as a beacon to help open up business doors where I needed the degree to carry me further in my career. I kept this motivation in the back of my head during my two-and-a-half years of completing my degree. This period of time pushed me to the edge physically, mentally and emotionally. Writing early in the morning, plus making sacrifices to not attend certain events and using that time to write was very important to me.

Drug trafficking to a Doctoral Degree

Hustling has helped shape my life in so many different ways. I will never forget receiving a phone call from my mom, as a sophomore in college, stating that I needed to come home ASAP. My attempt at living a double life had caught up to me. You see, on one end of the spectrum I was an athlete, scholar and motivator within my community. On the other end of the spectrum, I was involved in trafficking and other illegal activities that had caught up with me. As I hopped on the first

The Hidden Curriculum

plane that morning, I never wanted that plane to land in Cleveland, Ohio, but it did. I had to man-up to my involvements and had pending federal time and pending restitution to pay on money that I made. I had totally let down my family. Throughout the course of that weekend, the Man above intervened to look out for me. There was a woman, by the name of Mrs. Greenwood, who stepped in on my behalf. She and her family were some of the main victims of this crime of mine, who had the power to have me prosecuted to the fullest extent of the law; but she said no. She said no to prosecuting me because she already had a son locked up in jail. Mrs. Greenwood also saw that my ability to hustle could be turned in a positive direction. This was the "stepping stone" experience that has forever changed my life.

During the course of my illegal activities, I supplied people and organizations that would, in turn, make profits by marking up their own prices. Looking back at those experiences now, I see that I gained a natural skill to motivate and encourage others to achieve a goal which, in turn, helped me to achieve my own goals. I do not condone what I did during that time period, but the internal hustle I gained from within is what has helped me to have some positive success in my present life. I just learned to turn the negative hustle into something positive. This is one of the main reasons why I chose to write this book. My main motivation was to educate, enrich, and enhance people's lives so that they may achieve their goals. If I help people to achieve their goals then I naturally will achieve my own personal goal, which is servant leadership. At the end of the day, if I know that I have motivated or touched someone's life, then my living is not in vain.

Yes I am an educator, author, orator and entrepreneur, but the greatest lesson that I have learned didn't come from my formal education or degrees, but through life experiences that represent what I call the "Hidden Curriculum" of life.

The Hidden Curriculum

Chapter 1 Reflection Questions

1. How do you hustle on a day-to-day basis within your own personal life?

2. What are some areas within your life that you need to work on with a sense of urgency? What will be your plan be? Who will you hold as your accountability partner? How will you measure your success in moving with urgency?

The Hidden Curriculum

3. What is your mission statement and vision for your life?

4. Who or what occupies your time and space? Create a list and examine those people, places, and things.

5. What are your areas of strength? What are your areas of weakness? What are your specific plans to develop your strengths but improve your weak areas?

The Hidden Curriculum

6. What teachable moments have you had in life that created "stepping stone" or "stumbling block" moments?

7. What fears do you need to overcome within your own personal life in order to move forward?

8. What are five things that you have learned about yourself in this chapter?

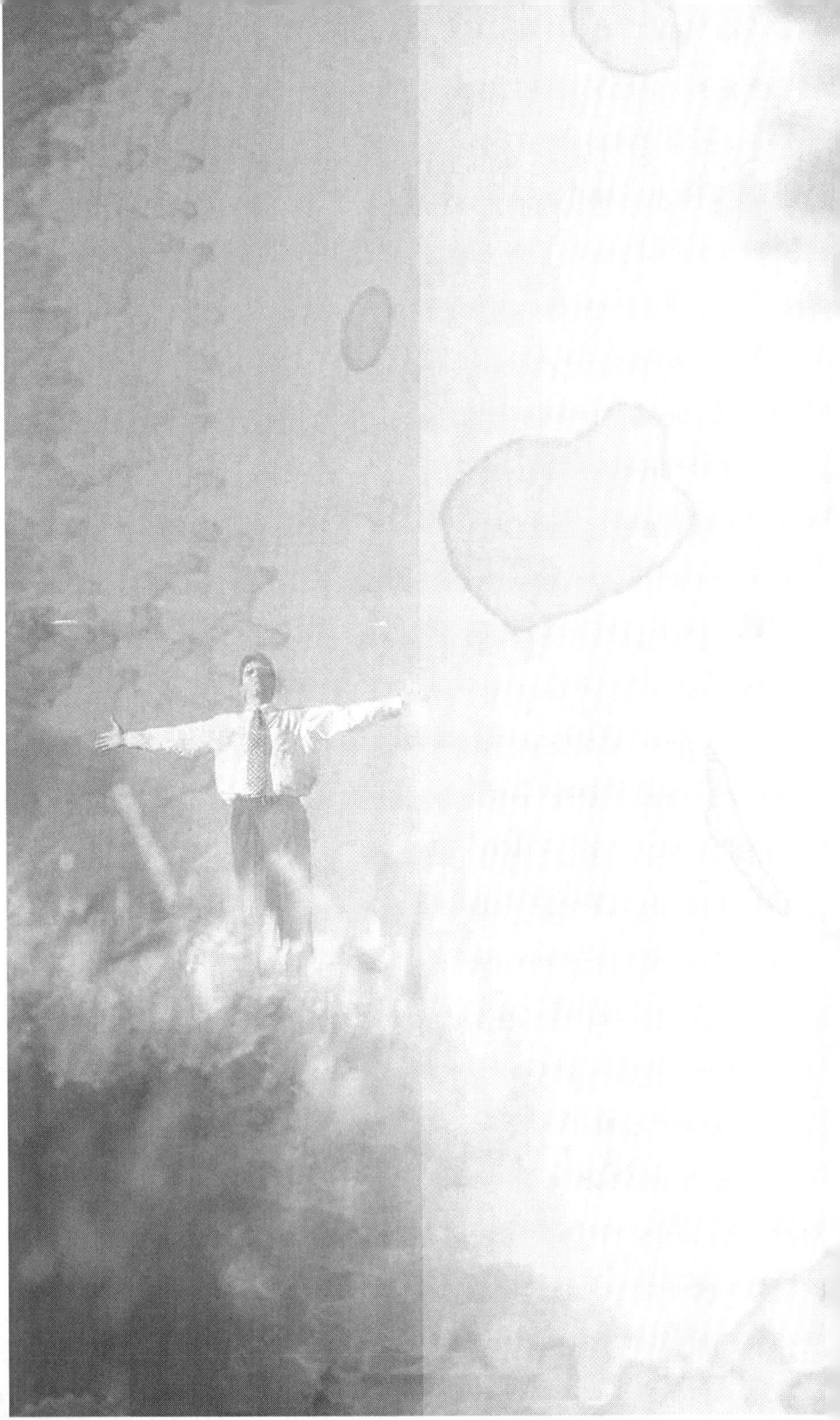

Chapter 2
Thinking Without Boxes

Outside the box to no boxes at all

When you look at today's society, starting from middle school through the collegiate level and even in the business world, the big push is to have people think outside the box. In recent years, this has been a big buzz word (Element 2). I believe there is an even greater concept; thinking without any boxes at all (Element 3). This concept envokes several reactions; discomfort, uneasiness, fear, trepidation, concern, and so on. Many people believe that to think without any boxes at all is a very dangerous place to be. I disagree with this notion. Remember, thinking is a mental action, cogitation, and/or a judgment. Thus, thinking has no parameters. It is endless.

Furthermore, if you look at the visionary leaders of our time like Steven Jobs, Bill Gates, Warren Buffet, Nelson Mandela, and many others, you will see they have created outcomes for themselves and

The Hidden Curriculum

carved a niche in society because, as visionaries, they thought without any boxes at all. They have built intellectual capital, social capital, and human capital. Ultimately, these components led them to financial capital within their lives. It is imperative that you begin thinking and living without any boxes at all!

If you begin living without any boxes at all, you will soon find out this helps you with the issue of procrastination. What I am trying to say is, you can begin to envision and act on what needs to be done to move forward and to really make a difference in society. There are certain questions you have to ask yourself: Are you living in a state of denial about the rewards or consequences in your life, or are you waiting for others to motivate you to move forward in society? Are you waiting for everything around you to become perfect in order to move forward in society, or are you trying to do everything on your own? Remember, perfection doesn't exist here on Earth. Additionally, no one person is an island. It takes a village to do a good deed in society, not one individual. These are things you must consider. As one of the great authors of leadership, John Maxwell, notes, "Talent is not enough." You can have a lot of talent. However, if you lack the drive, the gumption, and the fortitude to move things forward, you are wasting your talent.

You are either on the way or in the way

When you think without a box at all, you mimic a rocket ship. You propel into space. As you move into space, certain boosters begin to fall off so that you can continue to gain momentum and propel forward. Those boosters may represent people, places, and/or opportunities within your life. As you continue to excel in life, you will ascend into different orbits due to thrust. As you continue to climb, certain relationships may have to come to an end for you to continue your journey. It could be the current relationship you are in with a business partner, a significant other, or a spiritual shift. These relationships must change because they cannot handle the amount of orbit that you are in nor can you maintain your ability to ascend when you are holding on to dead weight. Sometimes people, opportunities, etc. are in your life for a season; not for eternity. Not everyone will understand your vision. Keep in mind that you cannot please everyone nor should you try to. The key is for you to realize when the season has ended so you can make the proper adjustments to continue your success.

The Hidden Curriculum

Furthermore, an indicator of a weak leader is someone who tries to please everyone. Inevitably, you go from thinking without any boxes, to thinking outside the box, to being constrained to thinking within boxes. You begin conforming to please people. You lose time and money. You can't fulfill others' expectations; you must fulfill what God has planned for you. If you try to please people, you will never live out the path that God has designed and laid out for you. Each individual is put here for a reason. As long as we are trying to please others, we are never going to realize what our reason and purpose is on Earth. It's important to take time out to figure what your path is supposed to be.

Maintaining no boxes

It is also very important for you to understand you have to protect certain things around you like your family, your calendar, etc. How many times have you wasted time, money, and energy attending meetings for the sake of meeting or attending several meetings and only being able to give ten percent because you are spread so thin? Wouldn't it be better to recognize the gifts you have been given and submit to those skills and abilities? Basically, why not commit to one or two organizations and truly give one hundred percent? God wants you

Thinking Without Boxes

to use your abilities in a specific way and for the specific goals He has set for you and your life. Although you have been blessed with many skill levels, maybe you should be focusing on one or two areas for a couple of years. Then you can hone those skills to be utilized in conjunction with your additional skills at a later date.

Be sure to take time out to control your schedule. You must learn it isn't necessary to attend meetings with individuals who don't share or fit into your vision at this time. You may have someone who wants to meet with you to share all of these ideas that don't fit or connect with your purpose at this time. That doesn't mean the ideas aren't good or viable, they just aren't aligned with your needs. Thus, you don't need to waste their time or yours discussing them. I have discovered that once you have been blessed enough to figure out what your purpose is, the minute you move outside this area for monetary gain, social gain, immediate gratification, or "being sold a dream", is when you deal with your biggest losses, frustrations, and not feeling appreciated but merely tolerated. It is very important that you move within your goals, dreams, passions, and purpose. This will help you move to the third element of thinking, without any boxes at all!

The Hidden Curriculum

The art of having no boxes

As I sit back and think about things and what one needs to do to get to this level, I realize that learning to think without a box is an art. There needs to be a class that guides you and helps you manage your life and shows you how to make the most of your life; specifically, to get you to the level of thinking without any boxes at all. I don't know too many people who start out their lives living it and doing it well. Most people never learn it. Those who do develop life management skills, do so over time. Life management begins with an awareness of time and the things we need to do to be good stewards of our time. The individuals who do this will advance their overall purpose in life, which helps them grow. They underscore their overall values which brings them fulfillment in life. They maximize their strengths and manage their challenge areas, thus becoming more effective people. They increase their happiness by doing things with and in their lives that provide motivation. This helps give them better mental, physical, spiritual, and emotional strength. These combine to help them increase their productivity and overall effectiveness in everyday society. By adding value to others, this increases their sphere of influence. All of these areas are of importance because they help you deal with not only time management but more importantly, life management. Successful life management helps you to achieve your particular goals, as well as achieving your particular dreams.

Choices

We all have choices that we must consider before we move forward. When I reflect upon the choices that I have made in my life, both positive and negative, one of the things that my choices have shown me is who I truly am; more so than the abilities that I possess. My choices show me what I believe in, what catches my attention, what I like, what I don't like, my positive attributes, my negative attributes, and my choices have humbled me. There have been times when I thought I was moving forward but, based upon my choices, I was pushed four steps back. Specifically, decisions about products to invest in to gain a quick profit, or allowing myself to be sold a dream about an idea that didn't move me toward my God-given purpose. As a result, I lost money, time, sleep, and authority over my life. Life choices will always intertwine with teachable moments. They will create stepping stones or stumbling blocks in one's life. It is all in what you decide. One other thing about choices is they are not always easy and they will often take you outside your

The Hidden Curriculum

comfort zone. When we move outside our comfort zone into uncharted territory, a lot of fear and uncertainty begin to affect us and our decisions. Don't make any decision hastily. Be sure to pray about your options and allow wisdom to give you discernment over your choices. When He tells you to move, go ahead and move. Don't hesitate.

Negativity is in your face, pushing you

No one likes to be pushed into a situation or against a wall where you have no choices at all. This is when we go into our fight or flight mode and react, instead of rationally thinking things through. Think of a time when you were pushed up against a wall or backed into a corner and you had to decide whether to come out swinging or to lay low. That is not a good position to be in. Remember that the choices you make in all relationships, whether they are platonic, romantic, or business, will change you and make you who you are. Again, people are in your life for a season, seasons, or for a lifetime. It is imperative to get a grasp on this in your life. We have all had a time in our lives when we held on to a relationship too long. It should have only been in our life for a season and we made it stretch into seasons because we didn't want to let go, to have to make the hard choice, or didn't want to be pushed

Thinking Without Boxes

out of our comfort zone. This causes you to lose a lot of time, energy, effort, and money. Adversely, think of a time when you should have worked on building a relationship but you cut the person off too quickly. Be sure to examine each relationship you are in and be sure to examine it openly and honestly. Are these relationships celebrating or tolerating us? What is the makeup of this relationship? Is this benefiting me? Is it keeping me stagnant? Why do I attend these meetings? Remember, the ultimate goal is for you to think without any boxes at all. So, there has to be a certain level of complement with people, places, and things to attain and push you towards your goal or purpose. Take time out to reflect upon the key areas affecting your life.

Purpose-driven plans versus people's plans for you

In the context of not pleasing everyone, you may need to include your parents, family, and colleagues. They have certain standards for you. Traditionally, people set these standards for you based on past experiences and behaviors. What you should realize is that your standards for yourself should always be higher than anyone else's standards for you. Don't allow your past experiences to always define who you are. You can utilize past experiences as building

The Hidden Curriculum

blocks and life lessons about what you should or should not do. You don't want your future to be overshadowed by your past. Part of thinking with no boxes at all is realizing that you can always evolve and change. The sky is the limit.

Let your discouragers be your motivators

Certain people will be quick to throw your past experiences in your face by telling you that you can't do this and you can't do that for various reasons. A prime example of this is when I was in the third grade, my teacher informed my mother that I asked entirely too many questions and because of my asking too many questions, they thought I had some emotional problems. This could have been a crutch or a stumbling block, but I chose to use it as a stepping stone. Expectations were placed upon me to be more than what my teachers told me to be. Through grace and time, I moved forward and got my undergraduate degree, my master's degree, plus I was the quickest in Tennessee State University history to graduate with my doctoral degree.

I challenge each and every one of you to determine who is putting standards upon you. Who in your life is telling you what to do in society based upon your past experiences? Who in your life is telling you what to do based upon your education

Thinking Without Boxes

level or lack of education? A prime example of this is Barack Obama. He has experienced adversity and other people putting standards on him for years. Besides being the first African-American President, many thought he was too young, hadn't achieved enough, or lacked the proper credentials to succeed. He had different expectations of himself and ultimately, achieved his goal to be President. Additionally, Michelle Obama provided him with a tremendous support system. She is an outstanding attorney, speaker, and educator in her own right. Additionally, her ability to lift up and support her husband has been instrumental in his success. They came together as one with united standards and realized their standards were of a higher calling. Thus, they have risen above any adversary who has come against them. It took him some time to be able to think without any boxes at all, but he has accomplished this task. He is making decisions and choices that have never occured in American history. This is not the easy choice. He is walking and leading the country into uncharted territory. The old adage stands true, "if you always do what you've always done, you will always get what you always got." Meaning, the road most traveled isn't always the best path or the correct path. This is a

The Hidden Curriculum

fundamental understanding that President Barrack and Michelle Obama have embraced.

No ceilings

Remember, helping people is more than making people feel happy. You can't complete your vision, goals, dreams, or aspirations unless you bring people along with you. As you bring people along, you then have a certain level of trust and respect that those individuals must have for you and vice versa. You have to push them, encourage them, empower them, and motivate them to achieve their goals; not just tell them what makes them feel good in the moment. One of the reasons I decided to write this book is that it further develops and intertwines with my purpose to educate, enrich, and empower people's lives so they can achieve their goals. This, ultimately, allows me to achieve my goals of service and leadership. We need to encourage and empower all of society from the upper echelon to the lower income individuals. I want to reach the people who have been put down, told they can't do something, told they are incorrigible, those who have been abused and neglected, put in group homes, and led astray. Everyone needs to be pushed. One class of society wouldn't exist without the others. We cannot get caught up in the sensationalism of the media and its portrayal of an "all for one and one for all mentality." We must work hand-in-hand to succeed. Ralph Waldo Emerson stated, "What lies behind us and what lies before us are tiny matters compared to what lies within us."

We are living in an era where boxes are being moved. Globally, countries are working together and creating alliances which has never happened before in the history of the world. It has never been about just black and white. This world is about people at large. It has nothing to do with color. We are one society, one world, one people. I challenge you to look where you are in life, what your desires are, and what it is going to take to get you to that point. Write this down. Once you have done this, you will begin recognizing and noticing the changes that are occurring in you and around you. By writing down and examining these areas, you can assess on a daily basis whether you are moving forward toward your purpose in life. Don't move selfishly. Consider how your choices and decisions not only affect you, but your family, and your purpose. You will have to give up something to achieve your purpose. For example, President Obama gave up a lot of his privacy to reach his goal to be President of the United States.

The Hidden Curriculum

Giving up in order to go up

What is the next level of realizing your purpose worth to you? What are you willing to pay? Sometimes, the longer we wait to pay, the greater the price may be. We can either pay now or pay later. What sacrifices are you willing to make regarding family, friends, or monetary gains? What are you willing to trade to get to the next level? We may need to push back immediate gratifications, or quality of life. Sometimes we have to trade the first part of our life for a better second part of our life. What are you willing to give up in order to go up? All great leaders have asked themselves these questions. The answers will change and evolve as you journey through life. You need to learn to travel light. Remember, you will always go through change. Although we fight change and don't like it, we must realize that change is inevitable. If we learn to embrace it, it can propel us to new heights and new horizons. It is possible to move from thinking inside the box, to outside the box, to thinking with no boxes at all.

Be sure to catch on to the wave of thinking with no boxes at all. It is how you should go.

Chapter 2 Self-Reflection Questions

1. In what areas of your life do you think inside the box?

The Hidden Curriculum

2. In what areas of your life do you think outside the box?

3. In what areas of your life do you maintain no boxes at all?

4. Who in your life is a true visionary? Why do you consider them to be a true visionary? What have you learned from them that you can apply to your everyday walk in life?

The Hidden Curriculum

5. Reflecting on your life thus far, what are some positive and negative choices that you have made?

6. What were the specific rewards or consequences of those choices that you made? What did you learn from those experiences?

7. Have there been moments specifically within your life where people have judged you because of your past experiences? Have there been moments where you have judged someone because of their past experiences? If so, then what did you learn from that/those particular situations?

The Hidden Curriculum

8. As you move forward within the continuation of your life, who would you like to bring along for the ride?

9. What is the next level of growth worth to you? What sacrifices are you willing to make to achieve that next level?

10. What is your mission and purpose in life? What is your plan of action to get there? What is your specific plan to get to that point?

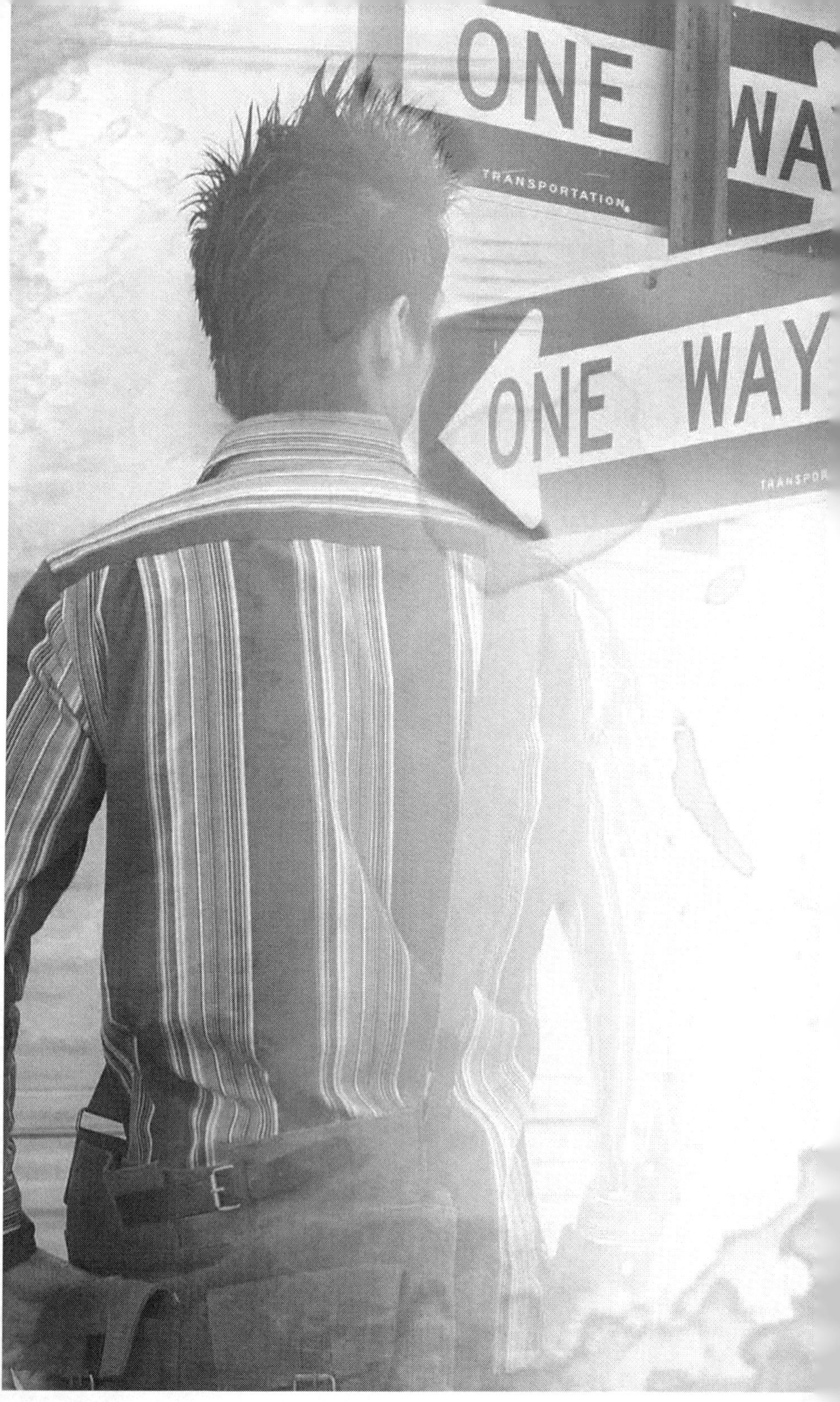
ONE WA
TRANSPORTATION
ONE WAY
TRANSPOR

Chapter 3
Learn To Lead Yourself So That You Can Lead Others

Throughout society, we have always had wounded leaders. This is a direct result of the leaders' personal lives being in chaos. Naturally, chaos in their personal lives leads to chaos in their businesses, organizations, or churches. The coach or leader is a direct reflection upon the spirit, habits, beliefs, and expectations of the senior leader and his/her influence over the atmosphere and culture of an organization. Some leaders don't take time out to address issues which have occurred in their past. These could be small stepping stone issues from childhood. The issue could have started out as a pebble which grew to a stone then into a rock and ultimately into a boulder because the leader keeps moving forward in life without addressing pertinent and underlying issues.

These insecurities, fears, weaknesses, and levels of emptiness inside the leader will manifest within the business, organization, or church when allowed to go unaddressed. Hypocrisy is an effect of

The Hidden Curriculum

unresolved issues. Hypocrisy is deception or playing a part that is false. Many of us are guilty of telling others what they need to do to change or better themselves, yet we are not willing to follow our own advice. We are not being the agents of change that we need to be or that we should be. I challenge you to look at yourself and how you position yourself within your leadership roles. How has not addressing your underlying issues not only affected you, but affected those around you? How has it affected your kids, your spouse, your colleagues, and your friends? The main thing to remember is that you aren't perfect and no one else is, either.

The H.O.W. process

You should utilize the H.O.W. process to address the issues at hand.

H stands for **Honesty**.

You must be honest with yourself about what is going on in your personal life and in your work life, including your career and organization. Are you living in a dream world or dealing with the realities around you? If you are living in a dream world, this can be detrimental to both you and the organization in which you are involved.

Learn To Lead Yourself So That You Can Lead Others

O stands for **Openness**

You must be receptive to constructive feedback. Once things become open and transparent to you, you might realize the life you have been living has been a lie or the life you have been living isn't the life you want for yourself.

W stands for **Willingness** to Change

This is the hardest step. It's easy to say, but you have to actually do it. You have to change your thought process, your habits and how you go about your day, what you think about, your expectation system, and how you organize yourself. As a leader, you cannot expect to lead others when you don't know how to lead yourself.

Image is everything

Keep in mind, within the first seven seconds that someone meets you, they will make eleven observations about you. This includes how attractive they find you, your socioeconomic status, determining how intelligent they think you are, etc. You do the same thing when you meet others. The image and perception you exude to others is important. Generally speaking, you do not see yourself as others see you. If you don't look at yourself realistically, you

The Hidden Curriculum

won't be able to see where your personal difficulties may lie. To be a good leader, you must be confident in who you are and what you are about. You have to be able to lead yourself effectively before you can effectively lead anyone else.

Furthermore, you must also take into consideration that you are harder on others than you are on yourself. It is easy to utilize two different sets of criteria when judging yourself versus others. It is common to judge others on their actions, what they do, and how they do versus ourselves and our intentions. As long as our motives are good, we tend to let ourselves off the hook. This scenario can play out over and over and over. Lou Holtz once explained, "Ability is what you're capable of doing. Motivation determines what you do. Attitude determines how well you do it."

Am I my own biggest obstacle?

The challenge is to find and make the necessary changes within you. To effectively lead yourself, you must have solid mentors (both male and female) to hold you accountable. These are individuals who may have already achieved the goals you are striving to attain. They are willing to guide you and give you insight into how they accomplished specific tasks and goals.

Learn To Lead Yourself So That You Can Lead Others

Discipline is another necessary component for your success. You have to make sacrifices to craft your discipline and yourself so you can reach to the next level. When you think the weight of the world is on your shoulders, it is important for you to remember that God never gives you more than you can handle. You have to step out in faith sometimes, however, in order to know that there are certain disciplines you should have and must develop for yourself and within yourself before you can lead yourself or others successfully. Self discipline is very important. Do you get up and exercise in the morning? Do you eat healthfully? Do you feed your spirit? Do you make arrangements to create structure and organization in your life? If you don't have these things in place it's ok, just start the process to get these boundaries in proper order. If you need help or assistance, then seek out people who can help you get there.

People are always watching you to see what kind of example you are setting. You may no longer be able to be around certain friends or continue certain habits because they keep you from attaining your goals. This refers back to some people, places, and things that are in your life for a season and may have already served their reason or purpose for you. Be prepared. When you are making these changes it

The Hidden Curriculum

may appear that you are under attack or that things get difficult before they get better. Keep in mind that there is a plan and a purpose in place for you. Self-discipline is an essential key, as well as having mentors in your arsenal, because two heads are always better than one.

Patience is another necessary component. Patience by definition is an ability or willingness to suppress restlessness or annoyance when confronted with delay. John Maxwell once said, "When you are foolish, you want to conquer the world; when you are wise, you want to conquer yourself." This is an area in my life, particularly this year, which I have really been working on. Sometimes in life when you achieve so much, so quickly, it becomes easy for you to take on an attitude of unrealistic expectations, and thinking that things should always happen in this manner, which is not always the case. What I am trying to say is that you take on a mindset of expectation. I have learned that obstacles and barriers are placed within our lives to teach us patience. Leaders must remember that the point of leading a group isn't to cross the finish line first, but to take people across the finish line with you. Leaders must deliberately slow their pace, keep others linked to them, enlist others to fulfill the vision, and lift people up to the next level. You can't

Learn To Lead Yourself So That You Can Lead Others

do this if you are always running ahead of your team or yourself. Learning patience and practicing patience can give you a new and different perspective on life. Patience may be the time when you are seeking that special someone in your life. For whatever reason, sometimes that relationship partner isn't brought into your life as soon as you'd like. Then when you least expect it or you are at your loneliest moment, God places that person in your life. He places that sunshine in your life to help you mend a broken heart or address other issues. This helps mold you and groom you to have testimonies later to share with others. It is through these trials and tribulations, as well as the personal tests of character, which create your testimony.

Energizers or Energy-Drainers

You must have people around you to whom you are accountable. People who lead themselves know that they can't trust themselves. They know a secret. Power can be seductive and they understand their own foul ability. To be a good leader and to deny this puts them in danger. An old Chinese proverb explains, "When you see a good man think of emulating him, when you see a bad man think of examining your own heart." Accountability is a willingness to explain our actions. Effective

The Hidden Curriculum

accountability begins long before you take action. It begins with getting advice from others. Once you get this advice, you can gain knowledge to make an informed decision and choice. This will help you navigate your destiny. As Helen Keller aptly put it, "Alone we can do so little; together we can do so much".

You are held responsible for your actions, and the actions of those you lead. Leadership is a privilege, not a right. Thomas Watson stated, "Nothing so conclusively proves a man's ability to lead others as what he does from day-to-day to lead himself." Self-examination is the key. How clearly do you really see yourself? How often do you reflect upon your situation and what you are trying to achieve? Once you can objectively see yourself, then you can determine what you need to do to leave your indelible mark on society.

Being real with yourself

Ask yourself what area you need the most help in right now. This question and the answer will change as long as you continue to address the particular areas that you may have. As you go through experiences in life, you have stand-out moments that show your true character by how you react in the heat of a situation. This is like the

Learn To Lead Yourself So That You Can Lead Others

scenario, "garbage in and garbage out". What you put in yourself comes right back out. Your character isn't made during these times; it's displayed during this time. Frank Outlaw observed, "watch your thoughts, because they become your words; watch your words, because they become your actions; watch your actions, because they become your habits; watch your habits, because they become your character; watch your character, because it becomes your destiny."

Character often shows others why they should follow you as a leader, who you are as a leader, and what you are really all about. Defining moments aren't the rule: they are the exception. What is normal doesn't work during a defining moment. One thing for sure, you will never be the same after a defining moment. As I stated in chapter one, my defining moment was when I was on the wrong path headed toward becoming another African-American male in jail. I had to face the fact that I had to be real with myself very quickly or my future was doomed. This is one of the reasons I wrote this book; to share lessons and experiences that you will not learn through the regular curriculum of a classroom. Life is deep and intricate. It is important for you to keep a journal of all of these types of moments in your life, both positive and negative.

The Hidden Curriculum

You never know when you might want to write a book or a set of memoirs for your children. Think about times when your heart has been broken either through death, or the breakups of platonic or intimate relationships. It is these moments that shake our lives that really shape our lives and who we are. These experiences toughen you, but you can't let them harden your heart.

Reflecting back in the day

In the fourth grade, my elementary school performed a play about Martin Luther King. I had decided that I wanted to play him and that no other role would suffice. It was a daunting challenge, but one that I wanted. I have since come to realize that it was through this experience that I discovered my love of public speaking, empowering people, and educating people. This was a great experience for me. Moments will stand out from your past, defining moments that push you forward or hold you back. Remember, the past doesn't have to predict our future. There are so many people who are going to remind you of who you used to be. You can't let these people hold you down or get you caught up in the past. Sometimes, you just have to lead yourself. This can be frightening. But you must trust in yourself and in the One who provides it all for us. You

Learn To Lead Yourself So That You Can Lead Others

must truly learn to lead yourself. Once you learn this, you can truly lead others.

I challenge you to look at your own personal leadership style on a day-to-day basis. How do you lead people? What is your level of self-discipline? What is your level of patience? Do you have mentors? In what areas of your life do they help you? Do your mentors hold you accountable? If yes, how do they hold you accountable? If you take time out to constantly and consistently evaluate these areas, then you will be headed in the right direction.

# The Hidden Curriculum

Chapter 3 Reflection Questions

1. What are some ways over the years that you have been honest with yourself and others?

2. What are some ways that you have been dishonest with yourself and others around you?

Learn To Lead Yourself So That You Can Lead Others

3. What are some ways that you have been totally open with yourself and others around you?

4. What are some ways that you have been totally close-minded toward yourself and others around you?

The Hidden Curriculum

5. What are some ways that you have made personal changes or helped someone else to make personal changes?

Learn To Lead Yourself So That You Can Lead Others

6. What are some ways that you have not made changes involving yourself or helped others around you to make changes?

The Hidden Curriculum

7. In what ways are you exercising discipline within your life?

8. In what area(s) of your life do you consider yourself to be undisciplined?

Learn To Lead Yourself So That You Can Lead Others

9. In what area(s) of your life do you consider yourself to be patient?

10. In what area(s) of your life do you consider yourself to be impatient?

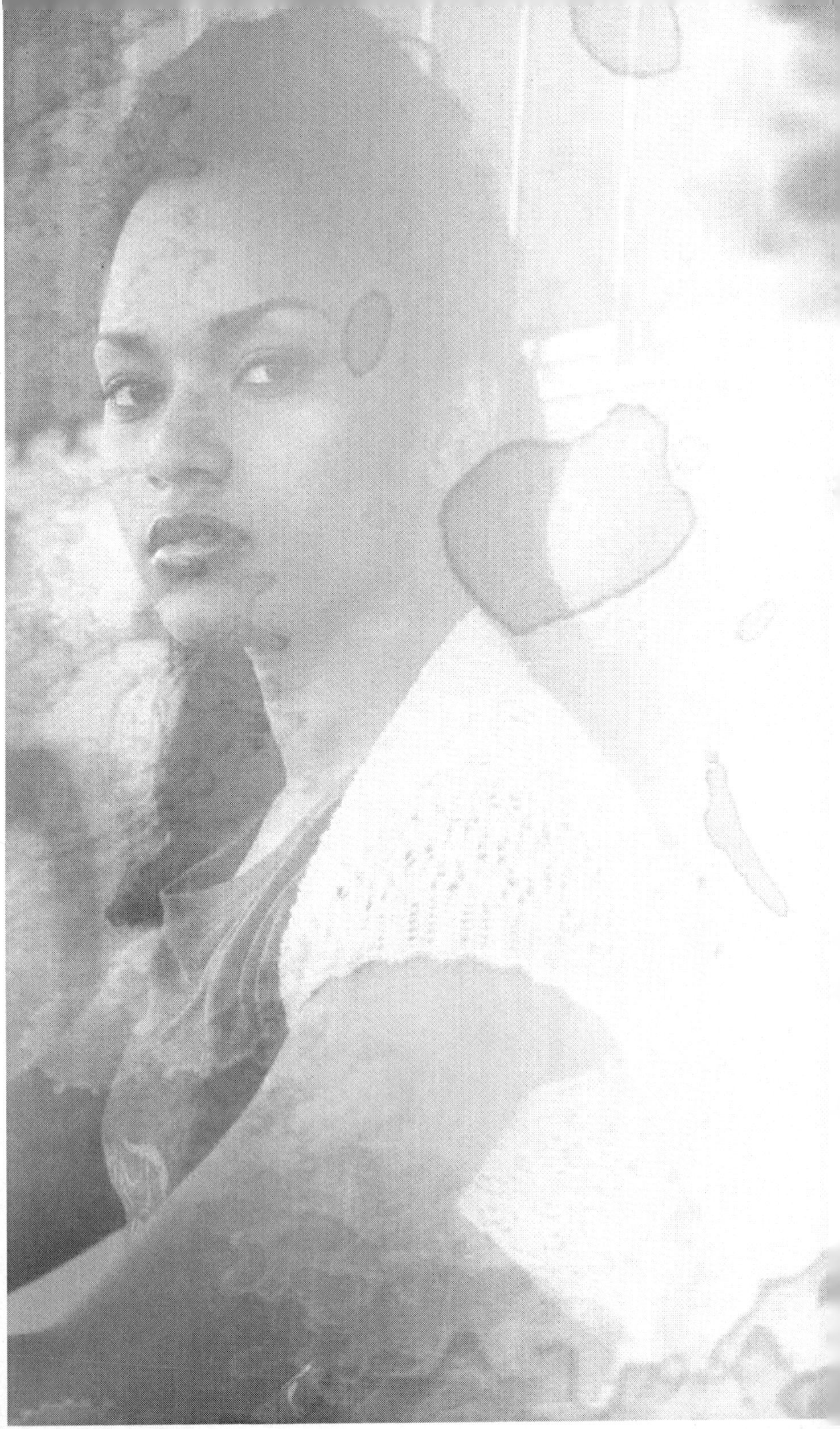

Chapter 4
Celebrated or Tolerated

What is celebrating and tolerating?

This is a very interesting thought. First, let's examine the meaning of toleration and celebration. Toleration is an allowance which is given to that which isn't wholly approved. Celebration is when you praise, extol, commend, or give praise to something or someone. As a leader, you can impress people from afar, but you impact them up close. This is an important and eye-opening fact that you must realize. I encourage you to get a pen and piece of paper and make a list of those individuals who merely tolerate you and those individuals who celebrate you. This has to literally be written down on paper and modified regularly. I challenge you to evaluate every relationship you have in your life with honesty and open eyes. You have to be able to clearly see the dynamics of your various relationships both personally and professionally. All relationships that are in your life have meaning. You don't want to continue to devote your time, energy, and effort to someone who doesn't reciprocate,

The Hidden Curriculum

appreciate, or celebrate you. Life is too short to not have people lift you up.

Those who tolerate you may include individuals who only see you when they need help, the haters in your life, or those individuals who only want to see you go so far. This is illustrated by the old adage, "Misery loves company". Other people who are miserable in their own lives cannot and will not lift up another person toward their successes. These individuals keep trying to remind you of your past, what they consider your limitations to be, etc. Don't let other people's selfish ways, attitudes, and motives affect you and what you are destined to do and be. I challenge each and every one of you to feed these individuals with a long spoon. In other words, keep them at a distance. Furthermore, keep in mind that it isn't the person, it's the problem. It's the problem that they have within themselves. You have to decide how to procede with this person. Do you want to completely cut them off because they are so toxic to your life? Do you need to entertain them from a distance? This is something that will need to be examined on a case-by-case basis.

People and Life Shifts

Again, someone can start off in your life celebrating you and then begin merely tolerating you.

Celebrated or Tolerated

This person might have served their purpose for a season in your life and you might have served your purpose for a season in their life. I know this may sound harsh, but it's not. As you achieve the successes and goals that have been set before you, certain individuals begin tolerating you through resentment, selfishness, or lack of understanding. Their behavior can go from consistent to inconsistent. Just remember, these changes aren't your fault. It is their issues, not yours, that cause this breakdown or change in behavior on their part. Quit blaming yourself for the mistakes and actions of others. Only take responsibility and ownership for your mistakes and actions. You must learn to separate the two.

In this process, you will find out a lot about yourself. Through this reflective and evaluative process, you may realize you have more people in your life who tolerate you versus those who celebrate you. It's imperative to re-evaluate your overall well-being and your own foundation and beliefs, if you find this to be true. As a leader, or one in the process of becoming a leader, you must have the ability to evaluate, self-reflect, and adapt. John Maxwell once noted, "The size of outstanding leadership appears primarily amongst the followers," so as a leader you have two common characteristics. The first characteristic

The Hidden Curriculum

is that you are trying to go somewhere and the second characteristic is your ability to lead others. Both of these are equally important.

Leading and Following

Whether you are a pastor, a leader in the community or within an organization, you must ask yourself this question: are people following what I am saying or am I just talking? Does your message really infiltrate the lives of others and motivate them to take action? This ability to have influence is what separates the leaders from the pretenders. The only way people will follow you is if they can celebrate your goals, your dreams, your aspirations, and/or your vision. You must possess the skill set and the ability to turn followers into leaders as well.

You have to constantly look to see if the people you are leading are changing, and growing. If they are changing based upon the information you are sharing, then they are celebrating you. They are celebrating your wisdom, your vision, and your involvement in their lives. If they aren't celebrating you, you must re-evaluate to find out why. A leader can only create opportunities when others are willing to change. This is when a leader functions as an agent of change. People have to believe in your abilities and your leadership in order for change to

Celebrated or Tolerated

occur and to be created within people. Good leaders aspire to teach people to have confidence in them (the leader). However, great leaders aspire to teach people to have confidence in themselves, not just the leader. Eric Hoffer says, "In times of change, learners inherit the Earth, while the learned find themselves beautifully equipped to deal with a world that no longer exists."

To be a good and effective leader, you must instill a level of expectancy. A great leader must create an environment or a culture of change, celebration, expectations, and commitment. You will create hope for people to succeed. Failure is not an option, excuses are unacceptable, and excellence must be a way of life. As a leader, you must create this environment. This doesn't mean you won't suffer disappointment or failure. But the true measure of a leader is how he/she responds during times of adversity, rather than during times of success.

Dessert times of life

It is easy to have great character when things are going your way. Some of the most important lessons you will ever learn are experienced during the most difficult times in your life. Martin Luther King, Jr., stated, "The ultimate measure of a man is not where he stands in moments of comfort, but where

The Hidden Curriculum

he stands at times of challenge and controversy." It is through these times of trials and tribulations, that you can gain insight, knowledge, and experience that may propel you towards your vision. It is important to not use issues from your past as excuses for your failure or lack of success. Everyone has a story of past hurt and disappointment. The things that you do in life have to be exemplified through excellence, not through mediocrity. You cannot spread yourself over too many areas. This is not beneficial or productive for you or the task at hand.

Being the change you want to see

Harold R. McAlindon said, "Do not follow where the path may lead. Go instead where there is no path and leave a trail." As an effective leader, you should set short-term goals, mid-term goals, and long term goals. These are the parameters by which you can measure your achievements, successes, failures, and then adjust accordingly. Success will never come to those who just sit back and wait. It's kind of like the old saying, "If you're not the lead dog, the view never changes." Dale Galloway once observed, "The growth and development of people is the highest calling of a leader." For an organization to succeed, the people

Celebrated or Tolerated

must be willing to not only change but be willing to grow. As a leader, it is your responsibility to grow and develop your people. If you fail to do this, your competitors will surpass you because you have become stagnant. The responsibility of a leader is to develop people, not only to be better employees but to be better people. If you merely focus on making your employees better employees and not better individuals, they will learn to tolerate you instead of celebrating you. With this philosophy, you may see some short term success, but failure will follow long term if you only care about the job-related aspects of the individuals and not for them as individuals. Core principles of development depend on a leader believing in his/her people and the people believing in their leader.

The next question you should ask yourself is, are people around me winning? Pat Riley, who has led two different teams to the NBA championships, said, "The way to measure whether you as a leader are doing a good job is 1) to measure your wins and losses, 2) through measuring your bottom line, and 3) through the subjective and objective visual analysis of how individuals are improving and growing. If individuals are getting better results, then I think the whole product is improving. The bottom line in leadership is always results. Leaders may impress others

The Hidden Curriculum

when they succeed, but they impact others when their followers succeed. If a team, department, or organization isn't being successful, the responsibility ultimately falls on the leader."

There is no such thing as a solo leader. No one person achieves success all on their own. They have had help somewhere along the way. Look at Julius Caesar, Louis XIV, Mahatma Ghandi, Abraham Lincoln, and Martin Luther King, Jr. These great leaders were inspirational and demonstrated strong leadership qualities in their own right. However, their successes and triumphs were due to the people who surrounded them, supported them, and believed in their vision. If you want to be a successful leader, you will need the support of many individuals around you. If you are wise, you will appreciate and acknowledge their contributions to your success.

The Art of a Leader

You as an individual should have your own dreams, goals, and aspirations. If people celebrate you, your character, and your vision, you will get ahead. Keep in mind that, as a leader, you will never get ahead until your people are behind you. When necessary you can lean back and they can help push you forward. When you move forward in the

Celebrated or Tolerated

correct manner, then people will surround you and propel you forward. As a leader, I have been guilty of thinking that I can handle it all. This is just not the case. In sales principles, you learn that you are only as strong as your weakest link. If you only rely on yourself, you have no other links in your chain. Great leaders surround themselves with people who excel in areas where they are weak. When I look back over my life, I realize that I have been extremely blessed. I look back at the mentors who have come and gone in my life. Although I have lost contact with some of my previous mentors, I realize that I have had support and assistance from individuals whom I have never met. Additionally, I realized that there have been several individuals who I knew helped me, but they never realized that they helped me and the impact they had on me. It should be your joy to express your gratitude to those unintentional helpers who brought favor into your life because they help to shape and guide your life. It is a gift to have people in your life who see a light within you that you might not see within yourself at that time. You must make a commitment to yourself and to God to inspire, encourage, and motivate others within our society.

Michael Jackson is a prime example of someone who helped change many lives. He knew some of

The Hidden Curriculum

those he helped and others only his spirit will know he helped. Not because of his music, but due to his generosity. While watching the BET Awards, I gained a new understanding and insight about him as a person and not just as a performer, celebrity, or icon. Michael is in the Guinness Book of World Records for doing the most philanthropic work in the world. Unfortunately, this is not something you will hear in the media. Through his experiences, his spirit lives on. He did touch others' lives through his philanthropy. Be sure to always evaluate where you are, what your goals are, and what you are saying in your actions and behaviors. Be authentic and always have a plan of action.

Do you have that guiding light to show that you are consistent in your leadership style and abilities throughout times of success and hardship? People watch to see if you become shaken but not stirred. If you can inspire, you can motivate. If you can motivate, you can educate. If you can encourage, you can enrich someone else's life. That is the power and purpose of a true leader.

Celebrated or Tolerated

Chapter 4 Reflection Questions

1. Create a list of people who celebrate you or tolerate you.

The Hidden Curriculum

2. Why do you feel people celebrate you?

3. Why do you feel people tolerate you?

4. What are some specific trials and tribulations that you have experienced that have allowed you to grow stronger?

The Hidden Curriculum

5. In what areas in your life do you feel that you need to grow?

6. Do you consider yourself an effective leader? If so, why? If not, why?

7. In what ways do you plan to improve and perpetuate lasting results in the future?

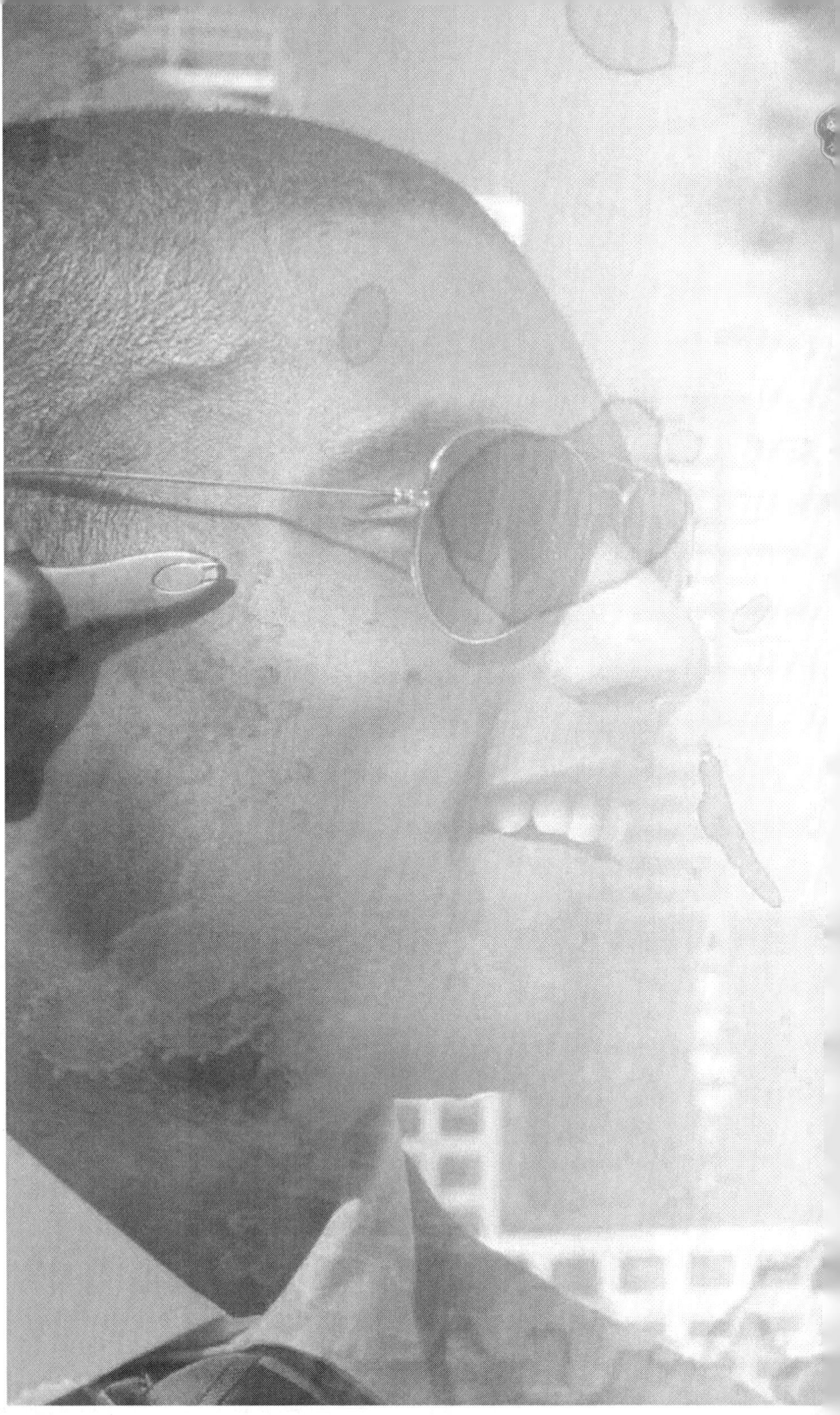

Chapter 5
Staying Ready

Getting Ready

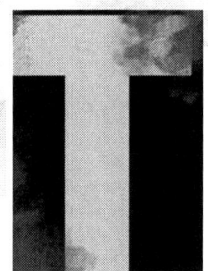

This expression is near and dear to my heart. The ability to be proactive instead of reactive is extremely important. What do I mean by proactive?

By definition, proactive means serving to prepare for, intervene in, or control an expected occurrence or situation. Being proactive can also mean staying presentable and ready for whatever may come your way. Whether you have one suit, one dress, or multiple suits and dresses, you should keep ready at all times. Part of staying ready is keeping yourself in good shape mentally, emotionally, and physically like I discussed previously. Furthermore, you should keep your resume up-to-date and always have copies with you on your flash drive or in print. Unexpected experiences happen in life; thus, the more you can get done early, or ahead of time, the better. You never know when something unexpected will happen and you can't get done what you thought you were going to be able to get done, due to this unforeseen circumstance. When you are

The Hidden Curriculum

reactive versus proactive, you not only lose time, but you also lose money, sleep, and opportunities. All of these increase the stress in your life. You should always take care of situations immediately and not wait until the deadline.

How have the positive and challenging experiences in your life marked you? Have you evaluated these experiences or are you still moping around and having a pity party? How have you dealt with these experiences? Experiences in and of themselves teach you nothing. However, evaluating and analyzing the experiences you have incurred teaches you life lessons. You can continue to have the same experiences over and over if you choose not to evaluate why they keep recurring. If you do the same thing over and over again you will continue to get the same result. John Wooden said, "Don't measure yourself by what you have accomplished, but by what you should have accomplished with your ability." Throughout life, you will have several experiences in your life that you don't understand. This is why you must evaluate and be honest with your assessment. Sometimes you must get the light off of yourself and look at everything around you.

Staying Ready

<u>You ready?</u>

Life is ten percent what happens to you and ninety percent how you respond to what happens to you. You must remember to ask yourself this question: Attitudes are contagious; is mine worth catching today? Does your attitude show signs of maturity and growth? This is a hard road to hoe. Detours in life that you don't understand can determine where your life leads you. It is through these experiences that we get testimony, and learn to grow and move forward. You must have a positive attitude toward detours on the path of life. These are what keep you strong, motivated, driven, and cause you to evolve and change. The difference between average people and achieving people is their perception of and response to failure. Ask yourself what is your response to success and failure within your life. Your response can make you or break you.

Keep in mind, some experiences can and will be very costly. They can affect you mentally, emotionally, financially, and spiritually. You must evaluate the problem, not the person in reference to the problem. Don't beat yourself up, but just find out what the core problem is and figure out how to keep it from happening again. These experiences put boldness in you so that you can rise to the

The Hidden Curriculum

occasion. You will learn to put pride aside to do what needs to be done because you deserve better.

There is a famous poem by Rudyard Kipling called **IF**. It simply states:

> If you can keep your head when all about you
> Are losing theirs and blaming it on you,
> If you can trust yourself when all men doubt you,
> But make allowance for their doubting too;
> If you can wait and not be tired by waiting,
> Or being lied about, don't deal in lies,
> Or being hated, don't give way to hating,
> And yet don't look too good, nor talk too wise:
> If you can dream – and not make dreams your master;
> If you can think – and not make thoughts your aim;
> If you can meet with Triumph and Disaster
> And treat those two impostors just the same;
> If you can bear to hear the truth you've spoken
> Twisted by knaves to make a trap for fools,
> Or watch the things you gave your life to, broken,
> And stoop and build 'em up with worn-out tools:
> If you can make one heap of all your winnings
> And risk it on one turn of pitch-and-toss,
> And lose, and start again at your beginnings
> And never breathe a word about your loss;

Staying Ready

If you can force your heart and nerve and sinew
To serve your turn long after they are gone,
And so hold on when there is nothing in you
Except the Will which says to them: 'Hold on!'
If you can talk with crowds and keep your virtue,
Or walk with Kings – nor lose the common touch,
If neither foes nor loving friends can hurt you,
If all men count with you, but none too much;
If you can fill the unforgiving minute
With sixty seconds' worth of distance run,
Yours is the Earth and everything that's in it,
And – which is more – you'll be a Man, my son!

Maintaining consistency and readiness

How often do you take time out to pause and evaluate yourself? It is imperative that you recognize the need to be still. What have you learned through your experiences? Are you moving forward or continuing to repeat the same mistakes? You must be willing to make the tough but correct decisions to move people through and out of your life from season to season. You must be ready to roll. Not everyone should take the journey with you. The question should be who is leaving and why. You can't wait around for people because, sometimes, they can hinder your progress. If you travel with

The Hidden Curriculum

others, you must wait on them, thus affecting your ability to progress and move forward.

Are you willing to stay ready? What is your reaction to people who don't want to stay ready with you? If you panic, this is a sign of weakness within you. Have you been waiting too long for people to move with you? John Maxwell noted, "Opportunity is nothing more than giving people what they need to go to the next level. A fit is something that puts them somewhere else that matches their strength. Potential is when people find out they have the ability to improve. Attitude is finding out if those people want to go to the next level with you. If the issue is opportunity or fit, they may very well rise to the occasion. If it is potential, they may be able to function at a lower lever. If it is attitude, they must change or they must go."

If you stay ready, you never have to get ready. This concept will allow you to open up and prepares you to achieve your goals. You must do what is necessary to accomplish the endeavors that are set forth for you. You don't have to listen to negative things that affect your spirit. Focus on the goal and vision that is in place to help you move forward. Don't miss your mark and then try to live vicariously through your children. They have their own talents,

Staying Ready

goals, aspirations, skill sets, and paths that have been laid out for them.

Buddha stated, "Do not believe in anything simply because you have heard it. Do not believe in anything simply because it is spoken and rumored by many. Do not believe in anything simply because it is found written in your religious books. Do not believe in anything merely on the authority of your teachers and elders. Do not believe in traditions because they have been handed down for many generations. But after observation and analysis, when you find that anything agrees with reason and is conducive to the good and benefit of one and all, then accept it and live up to it." Thus, I want you to know there is someone who believes in you.

I do believe in each and every one of you who have taken the time to read this book. My hope is that this book helps you have insight that will affect and change your life. I believe in you!

No matter what you have done, no matter what has happened to you in your life, no matter what other people say about you, no matter whether you are rich or poor, no matter your age or size, no matter your IQ, no matter your choice in music, no matter where you live, no matter your position... I BELIEVE IN YOU!

—Dr. Rubin Cockrell

The Hidden Curriculum

Chapter 5 Reflection Questions

1. What commitments are you ready to put in place to make positive long lasting changes within your life?

Staying Ready

2. Experience is the best teacher. What experiences do you feel have taught you the most about life?

The Hidden Curriculum

3. What abilities do you feel you personally have to help you progress to the next level?

4. Do you feel that attitude is necessary to bring about success?

Staying Ready

5. How often do you take time out to pause and evaluate yourself?

6. Are you willing to stay ready? Are you willing to remain prepared? How exactly do you plan to make the commitment to yourself to stay ready?

The Hidden Curriculum

7. What "Hidden Curriculum" have you discovered within your life?

Notes

Alan Cohen, Why Your Life Sucks and What You Can Do About It, (Alan Cohen Publications 2005)

Christopher Neck, Fit to Lead (New York: St.Martins Press, 2004)

Dale Galloway, Leading the Vision (Beacon Hill Press of Kansas City, 1999)

Eric Hoffer, The Temper of Our Time (New Republic, June 3, 1967)

Harold Maclindon, Getting the Most Out of Your Job and Organization (Amacom Publishing, 1980)

Hellen Keller, Light in My Darkness (Sweedenborough Foundation, 2000)

Jim Collins, Good to Great (New York: Harper Collins, 2001), 70.

John Maxwell, Attitude 101(Nashville: Thomas Nelson, 2003)

John Wooden, Wooden on Leadership (McGraw Hill 2005)

Katherine Meade, A Runner's Dream (Boutbound, 1998)

Marcus Buckingham and Donald O. Clifton, Now Discover Your Strengths (New York: The Free Press, 2001),6.

Notes

Marcus Buckingham and Donald O. Clifton, Go Put Your Strengths to Work (New York: The Free Press, 2001),6.

Pat Riley, The Winner Within (Kirkus Publishing, 1994)

Rudyard Kipling, The Letters of Rudyard Kipling (University of Iowa Press 2004)

Spencer Iverson, Donald Bradley, Floyd Williams, The 3 CEO's formula (Georgia:3CEO's,2008)

Thomas Armstrong, Multiple Intelligence in the Classroom, (McGraw Publishing's 200)

Thomas Holdscroft, The Pentateuch, (Western Book Company, 1966)

Thomas Watson, A Collection of Poems, (Edinborough Publishing, 1835)